P9-BBO-317

The Truth About Witches

by Eric Braun

illustrated by Robert Squier

PICTURE WINDOW BOOKS
a capstone imprint

Thanks to our advisers for their expertise, research, and advice:

Elizabeth Tucker, PhD, Professor of English
Binghamton University, Binghamton, New York

Terry Flaherty, PhD, Professor of English
Minnesota State University, Mankato

Editor: Shelly Lyons
Designer: Lori Bye
Art Director: Nathan Gassman
Production Specialist: Michelle Biedscheid
The illustrations in this book were created digitally.

Picture Window Books
151 Good Counsel Drive
P.O. Box 669
Mankato, MN 56002-0669
877-845-8392
www.capstonepub.com

All books published by Picture Window Books
are manufactured with paper containing at least
10 percent post-consumer waste.

Library of Congress Cataloging-in-Publication Data
Braun, Eric, 1971-
   The truth about witches / by Eric Braun, illustrated by Robert Squier.
      p. cm. — (Fairy-tale superstars)
   Includes index.
   ISBN 978-1-4048-6160-2 (library binding)
   1. Witches. I. Squier, Robert, ill. II. Title.
   GR530.B73 2011
   398'.45—dc22
                                    2010026901

Printed in the United States of America in North Mankato, Minnesota.
092010   005933CGS11

The Witching Hour

Abracadabra! For years, fairy-tale witches have been casting spells. They are magical, tricky women. We know them for their pointy hats and flying broomsticks.

Are fairy-tale witches real? Of course not! They are make-believe women in stories. They enjoy casting spells and making magic. And they continue to charm us today.

SPELLS

SHRINKING SPELL

LAUGHING SPELL

NO HOMEWORK SPELL

INVISIBLE SPELL

SMELLY SPELL

BURPING SPELL

SLEEPING SPELL

black cat

pointy hat

magic
wand

pointy nose
rotten teeth
hairy wart
pointy chin

broomstick

The Look of a Fairy-Tale Witch

In many stories, a witch is an ugly old woman. She has a pointy nose and chin. She has rotten teeth and a hairy wart on her chin. A hat sits on her head. And she flies on a broomstick. A witch often keeps a black cat as a pet. Sometimes she waves a magic wand.

In some stories, however, witches look like everyday women of their time. They might be pretty or plain, young or old.

In *Snow White and the Seven Dwarfs*, a beautiful witch is jealous of Snow White's beauty. The witch disguises herself as an old woman. Then she tricks Snow White into eating a poisoned apple. The apple puts Snow White into a deep sleep.

9

Witch Behavior

Fairy-tale witches are often evil. They trick people. The witch in *Hansel and Gretel* has a magic house. It's made of bread, cake, and candy. Hansel and Gretel are tricked into going inside. The witch locks up the kids. She hopes to eat them. But Hansel and Gretel outsmart the witch and escape.

Witches aren't always evil. In the story *Strega Nona*, a good witch has a magical pot that makes pasta. But someone else secretly uses the pot. He doesn't know how to stop the pot from making pasta. Soon there is pasta everywhere! Strega Nona saves the day by blowing three kisses.

L. Frank Baum's *The Wonderful Wizard of Oz* is known for its famous evil witch. But it also has a good witch named Glinda. She helps Dorothy return home from Oz.

Familiars

A fairy-tale witch often keeps a black cat, crow, or other animal. The animal is called a familiar. It is a spirit in the shape of an animal. A familiar helps a witch cast spells. A witch often lives with her familiar in a house in the woods.

HOCUS-POCUS, ALAKAZAM!

Spells and Charms

One of the most important things a fairy-tale witch does is cast spells. A spell is how the witch makes magic happen. To cast a spell, the witch might say a set of words. She might mix a potion of herbs and oils.

Spells can be used to help or hurt someone. In Hans Christian Andersen's *The Little Mermaid*, a young mermaid hopes to win the love of a prince. She asks an evil witch to turn her into a young woman. But the witch steals the mermaid's beautiful voice. The mermaid does not win the love of the prince.

Witch Stories

People have told stories about witches and magic for thousands of years. In an old poem by Homer called *The Odyssey*, the goddess Circe turns men into pigs. A goddess is like a modern fairy-tale witch. The hero of the poem, Odysseus, fights off the goddess' magic. Then Circe falls to her knees before Odysseus in defeat.

The Witch from
Hansel and Gretel

The Witch from
Snow White
and the Seven Dwarfs

Some of the most famous witch stories come from *Childhood and Household Tales*, by Jacob and Wilhelm Grimm. *Hansel and Gretel* and *Snow White and the Seven Dwarfs* are both from this book.

The Wicked Witch of the West is one of the best-known witches. She's from *The Wonderful Wizard of Oz*. This one-eyed witch makes Dorothy her servant. But in the end, Dorothy uses a bucket of water to make the witch disappear. The book was later made into a movie.

Witch Stories Today

People still love books, movies, and TV shows about witches. Probably the most popular recent story about witches is J.K. Rowling's *Harry Potter* series. The tale is about kids who go to school for witchcraft and wizardry. The series has been made into movies.

Most fairy-tale witches cause all sorts of problems. Their evil ways make things difficult for people. But in the end, people usually defeat the witches. Good overcomes evil.

Facts about Witches

- People who practice the religion Wicca are referred to as witches or Wiccans.

- Long ago, people believed real witches worked for the devil. Some people hunted and killed witches. Witch hunts were the worst in Europe. But in 1692, the people of Salem, Massachusetts, got caught up in one. They hanged 19 men and women they believed were wizards and witches.

- In the movie *The Wizard of Oz*, the Wicked Witch of the West wanted Dorothy's ruby slippers. But in the book, *The Wonderful Wizard of Oz*, the famous shoes are actually silver!

- In the movie *The Little Mermaid*, the young mermaid breaks the sea witch's spell and wins the love of the prince.

Glossary

cast—to cause a magic spell to take effect

familiar—a spirit that lives on Earth in the form of an animal, such as a black cat; it helps a witch with things like casting spells, spying on others, even household chores

potion—a mixture of liquids and other ingredients thought to have magical effects

spell—a word or words supposed to have magical powers

spirit—a supernatural being; ghost

Wicca—a modern religion in which people believe in a god and goddess and practice witchcraft

witchcraft—the practice of magic

Index

To Learn More

More Books to Read

Baum, L. Frank. *The Wonderful Wizard of Oz*. New York: Sterling Pub., 2005.

dePaola, Tomie. *Strega Nona's Harvest*. New York: G.P. Putnam's Sons, 2009.

Piumini, Roberto, retold by. *Hansel and Gretel*. Storybook Classics. Mankato, Minn.: Picture Window Books, 2010.

Internet Sites

FactHound offers a safe, fun way to find Internet sites related to this book. All of the sites on FactHound have been researched by our staff.

Here's all you do:

Visit *www.facthound.com*

Type in this code: 9781404861602

Check out projects, games and lots more at
www.capstonekids.com

Look for all the books in the Fairy-Tale Superstars series:

The Truth About Dragons

The Truth About Elves

The Truth About Fairies

The Truth About Ogres

The Truth About Princesses

The Truth About Trolls

The Truth About Unicorns

The Truth About Witches